BREEDERS' B

A KENNEL CLUB I

Miniature Pinscher

By Marcia P. Tucker

BREEDERS' BEST™
A KENNEL CLUB BOOK®

MINIATURE PINSCHER

ISBN: 1-59378-918-1

Copyright © 2004, 2006

Kennel Club Books, LLC
308 Main Street, Allenhurst, NJ 07711 USA
Printed in South Korea

PHOTOS BY:
Mary Bloom,
Isabelle Français and
Carol Ann Johnson

DRAWINGS BY:
Yolyanko el Habanero

Contents

MINIATURE PINSCHER

Meet the Miniature Pinscher

The Miniature Pinscher first emerged in Germany several centuries ago. There the breed was used as a highly efficient barnyard ratter. From archeological digs we have been able to learn of the breed's early beginnings as a member of one of the oldest family groups of dog, the Torfspitzgrupe. Broken down, *torf* relates to "turf" (or earth), *spitz* to a pointed muzzle and *grupe* to "group." Another breed we know today that also belongs to this group is the German Pinscher.

Although the colors and markings of the Miniature Pinscher certainly resemble those of the Doberman Pinscher, the Min Pin is certainly not a "small Doberman."

Skeletons of Torfspitz were recovered from lake dwellings in Switzerland, along with stone implements and other archeological evidence dating them back to 3000BC. This dog group was not limited to just Germany and the surrounding area but also was found throughout Europe and in parts of Asia. As ancient as the roots of the breed may be, though, more specific factual documentation only began in the past few centuries.

The Miniature Pinscher has been prized for centuries in Germany as a ratting dog. Its ancestry dates back thousands of years.

Like all breeds, the Miniature Pinscher developed from others. However, it is most certainly not a scaled-down version of the Doberman Pinscher, as is so often surmised. In fact, both the Doberman Pinscher and the Miniature Pinscher are likely to have descended from the German Pinscher, the oldest of these breeds. We know now that the "Min Pin," as the breed is often called by devotees, seems to have as its

The small Miniature Pinscher and the much larger Doberman Pinscher likely derive from a common ancestor.

ancestors the smaller smooth-haired German Pinscher, the Italian Greyhound and the Smooth Dachshund.

To dispel the myth about the Doberman Pinscher's being the ancestor of the Min Pin, the former was named after the tax collector and dog catcher Louis Dobermann, who did not breed his first real Dobermann (the name of the breed in Europe) until 1890, at which time the Miniature Pinscher had already been in existence. He was a skilled breeder and deliberately set out to create a working dog of medium size that would protect him. He actually stated that he wanted it to

There's not much resemblance between the Miniature Schnauzer and the Miniature Pinscher, but the two breeds did originate from the same family of dogs.

"look much like the five-pound Reh Pinscher but... fifteen times heavier and larger."

In Germany, the breed is known as the Zwergpin-

included both large and small varieties, and the Affenpinscher and Schnauzer were also part of this same family. There were also two coat types.

The Affenpinscher is another of the Min Pin's rough-coated relatives.

scher or Dwarf Pinscher. Stag-red dogs can also be called the Reh Pinscher, the name referring to the small red deer that used to be found in German forests. In the 1800s, the larger German Pinscher family

Not until the middle of that century did breeders decide to stop cross-breeding the different coat types. Of four specific types of pinscher mentioned by an author in 1895, the "short-haired dwarf pinscher" was clearly the Min Pin we know today. It is important to realize that the word "pinscher" does not denote a dog's heritage, but its method of working. It is actually a descriptive term, denoting a dog's habit of jumping on his quarry and biting it fiercely. It is also interesting to note that the word "pinscher" might be connected to the English "to pinch."

Although the Miniature Pinscher is generally believed to be a German breed, we should also keep in mind that the breed was depicted in French hunting prints from the 18th century. There have been several theories about the origin of the breed over time, but what is clear is that the Miniature Pinscher really came into its own in the latter part of the 19th century. Herr Hartenstein bought some pinschers in Swabia and took them to Wurttemberg, where he began a serious breeding program for black and tans.

It was in 1895 that the German Pinscher-Schnauzer Club was formed, with the aim of promoting the distinct pinscher varieties. The standard was set, with description of the correct temperament and a clear definition of colors. It was important that the Min Pin had erect ears. Tails were to be docked and coats were short and smooth, lying close to the skin.

The Miniature Pinscher became popular as the 19th century drew toward its close. The breed became especially popular in Germany between 1905 and 1914. The breed was first exhibited at Stuttgart in 1900, but until after 1918 was little known outside its homeland, except in some Scandinavian countries. It arrived in Sweden in 1905 and became firmly estab-

The Min Pin's ears must stand erect, whether natural, as shown here, or cropped, although some countries ban ear cropping.

lished there in 1915 when some very good-quality dogs were imported from Germany. By 1960, the

A big part of the Min Pin's appeal is his "big-dog" attitude packed into a small size that enables him to fit into almost any living environment.

Miniature Pinscher was the most popular toy dog in Sweden.

Slowly the breed spread through other European countries, though in Britain people were slower to recognize the many merits of the Miniature Pinscher. In 1949, Lionel Hamilton-Renwick traveled widely in Europe to locate good breeding stock, and he imported three red bitches, all of which had been mated before leaving the Netherlands for the UK. Because ear-cropping was banned in Britain, the youngest had been left uncropped so that she could be shown. Sadly, she died before whelping and the other two bitches both lost their litters, so Mr. Hamilton-Renwick went back to the Continent to seek a suitable high-quality male. In 1956, the breed was exhibited at the famous Crufts dog show for the first time; since then, its popularity has continued to increase.

In 1929, the Miniature Pinscher became fully recognized in America, too, when it was accepted by the American Kennel Club. It was here that the name "Min Pin" seems first to have been put into use. In the US, we call the breed the "King of Toys," denoting the high regard in which the

Min Pin is held as well as his "royal" personality. An important reason for the breed's popularity is its ideal size for those who live in apartments, and many an owner finds it difficult to restrict himself to only one! The Miniature Pinscher Club of America was formed in 1929 and, since then, the breed has enjoyed many waves of popularity. Now the perky little Miniature Pinscher has deservedly found its way into people's hearts all over the globe.

The Miniature Pinscher is a popular show dog. His signature high-stepping gait and confident presence catch the eye of many an onlooker.

MEET THE MINIATURE PINSCHER

Overview

- The earliest beginnings of the breed date back to 3000 BC, although the Miniature Pinscher is more commonly known for having developed in Germany in the late 19th century.
- The Min Pin is not a "small Doberman" and in fact existed before its larger relative.
- The breed was prized for its skills as a ratting dog.
- The Miniature Pinscher gained popularity in its homeland, which gradually spread throughout the Continent, eventually finding its way to the US and Britain.

MINIATURE PINSCHER

Description of the Min Pin

A spunky little dog with a sense of humor—that sums up the Min Pin nicely! This breed is full of energy and has a bouncy personality that can brighten up the dullest day. Owners must always remember that this is a breed whose not-so-distant ancestors were bred to keep farm kitchens free of rats and mice. Thus the fearless Min Pin can be perfectly capable of being a ferocious little monkey when he sees the need. He can also be a bit of a barker, so teach him from the start that you

The Min Pin is a lively dog with a look that implores his owner, "Let's do something fun!"

will not tolerate more than is necessary.

The Min Pin may be the "King of Toys," but it is important to teach him that he is not the king of the home. The American Kennel Club's breed standard describes him as having "fearless animation, complete self-possession" and "spirited presence." The European standard says that he is "Lively, spirited, self-assured and evenly tempered" and that these qualities make him an agreeable family and companion dog.

The Min Pin, called the "King of Toys," certainly feels that he is king over his domain. He is very observant and alert, keeping a close watch over his territory.

In appearance, we all know that the Miniature Pinscher is small, but he is not as tiny as some of the other toy breeds, for he measures 10–12.5 inches in height at the withers. Show dogs in the US will be disqualified from competition if over or under those measurements. The weight for the Min Pin is about 9–13 pounds.

Characteristic of this breed is its precise hackney gait, a high-stepping

The Min Pin has a muscular, compact body with nothing in excess. The tail is traditionally docked in the US.

An accepted color, but one not seen too often, is blue. Although a pretty color, the blue color does carry with it the predisposition to certain skin and coat problems. Breeding for healthy blues must be done with extra care.

action in which the front legs move straight forward in front of the body and the feet bend at the wrists. In essence the Min Pin is a trotter, with a ground-covering, relaxed, fluent movement with strong drive from behind. The feet are cat-like, the nails dark.

The narrow head of the Min Pin is held proudly and is somewhat elongated, rather than being short and round as is the case with many other toy breeds. The muzzle is rather strong and is proportional to the skull. The eyes are black or nearly so. They are neither too round and full nor too small and slanting. The nose is black, although in chocolate- and blue-colored Min Pins it may be self-colored. Ears are set on high and, in countries where cropping is allowed, they may be cropped or uncropped. In America they must stand erect from base to tip, but in Britain and on the Continent they may be either erect or

dropped. Teeth meet in a scissors bite.

In general, the Min Pin has a compact, square body with a level back, which can slope slightly to the rear. The well-sprung rib cage is deep rather than barrelled, and the belly is moderately tucked up. The tail is a continuation of the topline, carried high and customarily docked short. In Europe, "natural" tails are favored. This is a smooth-haired breed, the short coat straight, lustrous and closely adhering to the body, which is uniformly covered with hair.

This brings us to color, which can be black, blue, chocolate or solid red of various shades. The markings on the first three colors are clearly specified in the breed standard. The AKC standard states: "Solid clear red. Stag red (red with intermingling of black hairs). Black with sharply defined rust-red markings on cheeks, lips, lower jaw, throat, twin spots

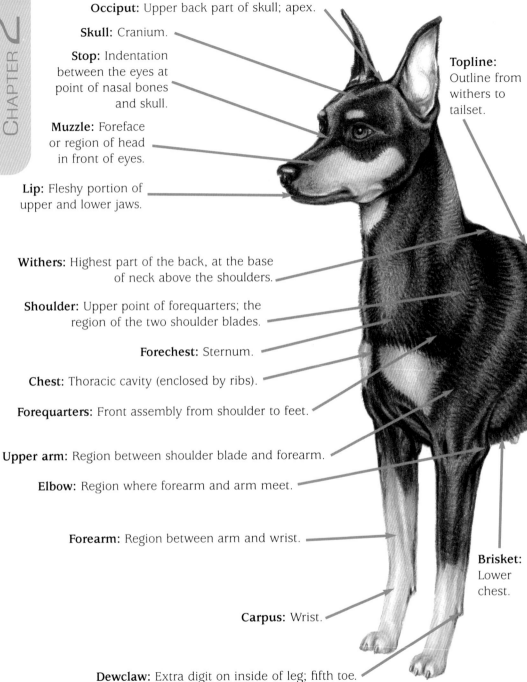

Occiput: Upper back part of skull; apex.

Skull: Cranium.

Stop: Indentation between the eyes at point of nasal bones and skull.

Muzzle: Foreface or region of head in front of eyes.

Lip: Fleshy portion of upper and lower jaws.

Topline: Outline from withers to tailset.

Withers: Highest part of the back, at the base of neck above the shoulders.

Shoulder: Upper point of forequarters; the region of the two shoulder blades.

Forechest: Sternum.

Chest: Thoracic cavity (enclosed by ribs).

Forequarters: Front assembly from shoulder to feet.

Upper arm: Region between shoulder blade and forearm.

Elbow: Region where forearm and arm meet.

Forearm: Region between arm and wrist.

Brisket: Lower chest.

Carpus: Wrist.

Dewclaw: Extra digit on inside of leg; fifth toe.

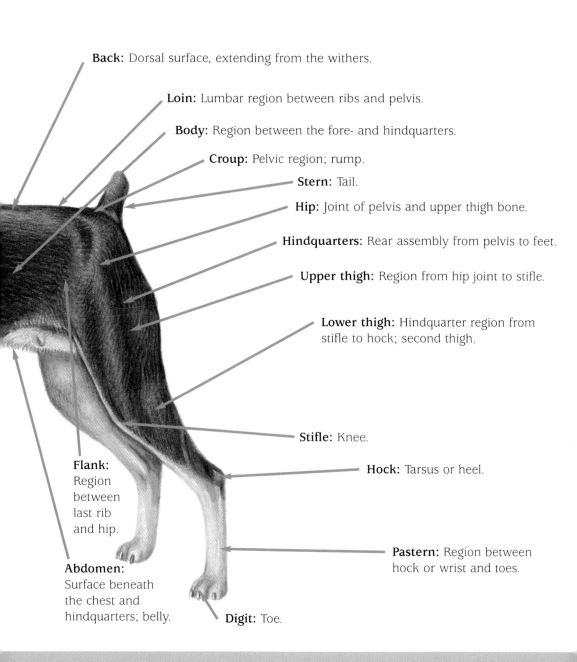

Back: Dorsal surface, extending from the withers.

Loin: Lumbar region between ribs and pelvis.

Body: Region between the fore- and hindquarters.

Croup: Pelvic region; rump.

Stern: Tail.

Hip: Joint of pelvis and upper thigh bone.

Hindquarters: Rear assembly from pelvis to feet.

Upper thigh: Region from hip joint to stifle.

Lower thigh: Hindquarter region from stifle to hock; second thigh.

Stifle: Knee.

Hock: Tarsus or heel.

Flank: Region between last rib and hip.

Pastern: Region between hock or wrist and toes.

Abdomen: Surface beneath the chest and hindquarters; belly.

Digit: Toe.

above eyes and chest, lower half of forelegs, inside of hind legs and vent region, lower portion of hocks and feet. Black pencil stripes on toes. Chocolate with rust-red markings the same as specified for blacks, except brown pencil stripes on toes. In the solid red and stag red a rich vibrant medium to dark shade is preferred. Disqualifi-

The chocolate color carries the same rust-red markings as seen on the black.

cations: Any color other than listed. Thumb mark (patch of black hair surrounded by rust on the front of the foreleg between the foot and the wrist; on chocolate, the patch is chocolate hair). White on any part of dog which exceeds one-half inch in its longest dimension."

And to sum up this remarkable little character, as the American Kennel Club has so aptly said of the Min Pin, "You should find dynamite in a small package, or something is wrong."

The AKC breed standard is the "yardstick" against which show dogs in the US are measured. The diminutive Min Pin is put up on a table during judging, enabling the judge to give the small dog a thorough evaluation.

DESCRIPTION OF THE MIN PIN

Overview

- The breed standard, devised by the breed's parent club and approved by the AKC, describes the ideal Miniature Pinscher. The standard explains in detail the desired physical conformation, character and movement, as well as breed faults and disqualifications.
- The Min Pin is small in stature and is classified in the AKC's Toy Group.
- The Min Pin's hackney gait is a breed hallmark.
- Ears are erect, whether natural or cropped. Ear cropping and tail docking are done in the US, but banned in other countries.
- The coat is short and lies smooth, colored in black, blue, chocolate or red, with rust-red markings where appropriate.

MINIATURE PINSCHER

Are You a Min Pin Person?

It really doesn't matter what size or shape you are, and your dog couldn't care one bit if your ears are large or small, pricked or even dropped. What matters if you are a Min Pin owner is that you are quick enough to keep up with this alert, intelligent little being that will fast become an important part of your life.

If you enjoy training, or teaching an odd trick or two, you will have a willing learner. And you will certainly

The Min Pin is the companion of choice for someone who wants a small-sized house dog with superb intelligence and a joyful (albeit a little mischievous!) demeanor.

need a sense of humor so that you can join in your Min Pin's merriment when he decides to play a trick on you. This might be fairly frequent, so watch out! Also, if you like acting the clown, your performance might just be overshadowed by that of your dog, who loves to be in the limelight and enjoys lots of applause. But if you are perhaps a little stubborn from time to time, you will have something in common with your Min Pin!

Because the Min Pin is small and does not take up too much space in the home, many owners elect to own more than one. They can even be walked together on a special lead like this one.

Of course, you can live in an enormous mansion and your Min Pin will probably be very pleased about that, because he is inquisitive and will love investigating every nook and cranny. Equally, if you are a city-dweller and live in an apartment, you can be sure your adaptable little four-legged friend will fit in somewhere. Of course, you will need to go out for walks with your Min Pin and you must be the kind of owner who will keep his dog under strict supervision;

Miniature Pinschers have proven good therapy dogs for hospitals and nursing homes. A visit and a cuddle with this little charmer is sure to brighten anyone's day.

otherwise, the dog is likely to get into trouble of one sort or another! Knowledgable Min Pin owners restrict their dogs to being on their leashes when in public places, which could be a law in your hometown. Actually, if there is a bit of Sherlock Holmes in your character, this will stand you in good stead because Min Pins will always be the first to take advantage of an open door or gate so they can go off to explore! With this in mind, it is essential to always keep an eye on your Min Pin and create an escape-proof environment, which is a much safer option than having to hunt for your little explorer if he runs off to follow his nose.

It is to be hoped that you are a tidy person. If you leave things lying around the house, you can be certain that they will soon be missing. Small objects especially can be swallowed and cause serious problems,

even death, so keep everything out of harm's (and your Min Pin's) way.

Your love of hairdressing will have to go by the wayside, for there is but one style in which you can groom your Min Pin. You have chosen a breed that needs little grooming, but you will enjoy giving him a good brisk brushing every couple of days or so. You must be someone who is prepared to devote time and attention to your dog, for a Min Pin needs plenty of socialization from an early age. Spoiling, however, is not recommended, because he can become something of a temperamental tyrant if allowed to do so.

If there are children in your life, a Min Pin might or might not be a good choice of breed. A lot will depend on how you have brought up your own offspring. If they have been taught responsible dog ownership and have

If you are interested in showing a dog, the Min Pin is a good breed with which to start. He is easy to maintain and transport, and he doesn't need much help to put on a great performance in the ring.

Min Pin owners appreciate their breed's portability, while the Min Pins appreciate being able to go most anywhere with their favorite people.

learned to treat dogs gently, then your Min Pin will probably love them. On the other hand, if your kids like rough-and-tumble play, and expect to include your precious Min Pin in this type of activity, then you should look for another breed. If you and your children have plenty of patience and understanding, always keeping in mind that this is only a very small dog, and if your children allow your Min Pin to approach them, rather than the other way around, you will have a recipe for family success.

Despite his small size, the Miniature Pinscher does require exercise. Daily walks will benefit both of you while strengthening your dog-owner bond with quality time spent together.

ARE YOU A MIN PIN PERSON?

Overview

- The Min Pin person is fortunate to have chosen a conveniently sized breed that can adapt to most any living environment.
- The Miniature Pinscher person has time to care for his dog, including exercise, training and grooming, and is willing to give the Miniature Pinscher the attention that he needs.
- The Miniature Pinscher person has a sense of humor and appreciates his dog's playful nature.
- The Miniature Pinscher person makes his dog's safety a top priority, always keeping in mind the breed's inquisitive nature.

Selecting a Min Pin Breeder

Depending on where you live, you may or may not have a wide selection of breeders from which to choose. But please don't rush in and buy from the nearest breeder with the first available litter of Min Pin puppies, only later to regret your decision. Look around carefully and, if necessary, wait a while longer to buy from the breeder of your choice.

Prospective puppy buyers should always keep foremost in their minds that there are many types of breeder,

Min Pins and their handlers finishing up in the ring. One of the best places to find a good breeder is at a dog show. Reputable breeders are eager to show off the quality of their efforts by exhibiting their dogs.

some with the breed's best interest at heart, others more profit-motivated and less dedicated to the breed's well-being. It is essential that you locate one that has not only dogs you admire but also breeding ethics with which you can agree. Sadly, in all breeds there are invariably some who are simply "in it for the money" and these you must certainly avoid.

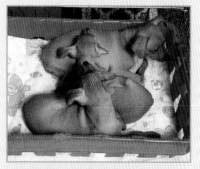

Visit the area where the pups are kept, as the breeder should provide clean, cozy living quarters for the litter. Most breeders allow visitors several weeks before the pups are ready to go to new homes.

That said, there are many good breeders around, and if you look carefully you will find just such a person. If you can be personally guided by the AKC or the Miniature Pinscher Club of America (MPCA), that is perhaps ideal, as member breeders must adhere to a Code of Ethics. You still need to be sure that the breeder's standards of care are what you expect. You must be certain that the breeder fully understands his breed and makes careful choices in his breeding program, taking into consideration

All puppies look sweet, but don't fall in love with every one that you meet! Your brain, not just your heart, must play an important role in your decision.

each dog's pedigree, health and overall soundness.

The breeder you select may be someone who breeds from their home, where the puppies will have hopefully been brought up in the house and will be familiar with all the activities and noises that surround them. However, the breeder may run a larger establishment, in which the litter has perhaps been raised in a kennel situation. Still, if you have chosen wisely, the puppies will have had lots of contact with people and exposure to a variety of sounds. Even some of the larger breeding establishments whelp litters inside the home; this is infinitely better than the puppies' being raised entirely in a kennel environment, especially for small breeds such as the Miniature Pinscher.

However large or small the breeding establishment, it is important that the conditions in which the puppies are raised are suitable. All areas should be clean, and the puppies should be well supervised in a safe, friendly environment. All of the puppies should look in tiptop condition and temperaments should be sound, full of fun with plenty of confidence. However, if you take your children along to visit the litter, always remember that you should allow the Min Pin puppies (and adults) to approach them, rather than the other way around. For your first visit to the breeder, do yourself this favor: leave the kids and your checkbook home. You will make a much wiser decision if you follow this advice.

The breeder should be perfectly willing to show you the dam, and it will be interesting for you to take careful note of her temperament and how she interacts with her offspring. If the dam is not available for you to see, be warned that this might be a

Now this is love! Some fanciers truly devote their lives and homes to their favorite breed.

CHAPTER 4

sign that the litter was not born on the premises, but has been brought in to be sold. In such a case, move on!

As for the stud dog, it is likely that he will not be available, for he may well be owned by someone else. A careful breeder may travel hundreds of miles to use a particular dog's stud services. Nonetheless, most dedicated breeders will at least be able to show you a picture of the

The breeder should allow you to meet the dam of the litter; if not, you should ask to see her. Frequently the sire will not be on the premises, but the breeder should have photos and information to share with you.

sire, as well as show you his pedigree and tell you about him. Ideally such a photograph will show him winning at a show as opposed to playing in the back yard.

A good show breeder usually keeps his very best puppies to show himself, or place them with other show breeders. Realize that you may not have the choice of an entire litter, but perhaps only one or two puppies.

A well-chosen breeder will be able to give the new puppy owner much useful guidance, including advice about feeding. Breeders should give a small quantity of food to each new owner when the puppies leave for new homes. In any event, the breeder should always provide written details of exactly what type and quantity of food is fed, and with what regularity. You will of course be able to change this as time goes on, but the change must be gradual.

A good breeder will tell you what vaccinations the puppy has received, and any relevant documentation (pedigree, registration papers, seller's contract and guarantee) should be transferred at the time of purchase. Details about the puppy's worming routine must also be made clear. Some breeders also provide temporary insurance coverage for the puppy. This is an especially good idea, and the new owner can subsequently decide whether or not to continue with this particular policy.

If you want life with your Min Pin to flourish, don't be hasty in your selection! Take time to research the breed, seek out the most suitable breeder and decide which puppy is your perfect match.

SELECTING A MIN PIN BREEDER

Overview

- To find a reputable breeder, write, phone or email the American Kennel Club or the MPCA for contacts. Online you can go to www.akc.org and www.minpin.org for more information.
- Know what to expect from a quality breeder and be patient in your search. Don't lose your heart to the first puppy that you meet and make a rushed decision.
- Be sure to get the important documentation including pedigree, sales agreement, health clearances, registration papers and vaccination records.
- A good breeder will be a source of help and information throughout your dog's life, so appreciate his knowledge and experience.

Finding the Right Puppy

So, do you truly feel that you have carried out sufficient home-work about the breed? Have you also done thorough research into which breeder is likely to provide you with the Min Pin that you feel will suit you best? OK, now you can make preparations to have your long-awaited Min Pin join you in your home. It is likely that the breeder will have allowed you to visit the litter beforehand, perhaps at five or six weeks of age, but you must

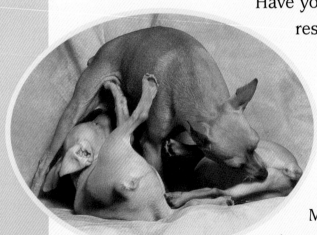

A caring mom and some of her brood. Mothering a litter of puppies takes constant energy and attention from both the dam and the breeder.

expect to wait another few weeks before the puppy is ready to leave his dam and siblings.

A healthy puppy should strike you as being clean, without any sign of discharge from the eyes or nose. His rear end should be spotless, with no sign of loose bowels. Although any puppy's nails can be sharp, they should not be overly long, indicating that the breeder has clipped them as necessary.

Min Pin pups of the same color resemble each other very closely. As long as all pups are healthy, your selection of a pet pup should be based on personality and temperament rather than looks.

The coat should clearly be in excellent condition, shiny and vibrant, and there should be absolutely no sign of parasites. Parasites such as fleas and lice cannot always be seen easily but will be indicated by the puppy's scratching, and you might notice a rash.

Scratching, though, does not always mean that there is a parasitic or skin condition, for it can also be associated with teething. In this case, the puppy will only scratch around

Miniature Pinschers are not large dogs, so you can appreciate how tiny they are as puppies. The breeder and any visitors to the litter must handle them with care.

his head area. When the second set of teeth have come through so that the gums are no longer sore, this scratching will stop. Scratching might also be connected with an ear infection, so a quick look inside your new puppy's ears will ensure that there is no build-up of wax, and there should be no odor from the ear. Of course, a good breeder will have checked that the puppy is in good health before offering him for sale.

Since all pure-bred dogs suffer from hereditary conditions, contact the Miniature Pinscher Club of America to find out about screening requirements for breeders, such as progressive retinal atrophy (PRA), hip dysplasia, Legg-Perthes-Calves disease, hernias, deafness, etc. Find out from the breeder whether or not the necessary hereditary tests have been carried out. You must ask to see written proof of the results and take note of the dates on which any tests were done; a good breeder will gladly show you this documentation.

Most puppies are outgoing and full of fun, so do not take pity on the overly shy one who hides away in a corner. Your puppy should clearly enjoy your company when you come for a visit, and this will make for a long-term bond between you. When you go to select your puppy, you should bring along the members of your immediate family with whom the puppy will spend time at home. It is essential that everyone in the family agrees with the important decision you are about to make, for a new puppy will inevitably change your lives.

The author is confident that you will have done plenty of research about the breed long before reaching the stage of having a new

Miniature Pinschers are house dogs, not dogs to be isolated outdoors or in a kennel. Look for a breeder who keeps his dogs and pups in the home as part of the family.

CHAPTER 5

puppy enter your lives. In addition to this book, there is much written on the breed, as well as many useful and entertaining web sites designed by breed clubs and individual fanciers. Along with learning how to care for a Min Pin, you may enjoy researching the breed's history and uncovering other fun facts.

Breed clubs are important sources of help and information. Some even publish their own leaflets and newsletters about the breed, and might even publish a book of champions so that you can look back to see what your puppy's famous ancestors actually looked like. There are also weekly or monthly canine newspapers and magazines, though you may

"These dogs don't look like us!" Curious Min Pin puppies get some early socialization by observing their canine neighbors from behind the security of their fence.

have to subscribe to them, as they are not always readily available at stores and newsstands.

For those who have access to the Internet and decide to look up breed information there, a word of advice: I urge you not to trust all that you read! These days anyone can set up a web site and can write whatever they like, even though they may not have a sufficiently firm knowledge of the breed or may be driven by their own self-centered agendas. Sites for which you find links on the MPCA and AKC sites should be honest sources of information from experienced and ethical Min Pin people.

Finally, it is a good idea to become a member of at least one Min Pin or all-breed club. In doing so, you will receive notification of breed-specific events in which you may like to participate, thus providing further opportunities to learn about the Miniature Pinscher and meet people in the breed.

FINDING THE RIGHT PUPPY

Overview

- Visit the litter to see the puppies firsthand. You are seeking healthy, sound puppies. Look for signs of good overall condition, such as bright eyes, shiny coats and solid little frames.
- Ask the breeder about hereditary conditions in the breed, as well as proof that the litter's parents have been tested for and cleared of any problems.
- Make sure that all family members are ready for the puppy and play a part in the selection.
- Be fully prepared by exploring various sources of information on the Min Pin. Contact a breed club and consider becoming involved.

CHAPTER 6

Welcoming the Min Pin

The day that your Min Pin puppy joins you in your home will be one of great excitement. Although you're not adopting a large dog, you will still need to make sure that everything is just as it needs to be to give your puppy the very best start. His sleeping quarters must be planned carefully, on a slightly raised surface, totally away from any draft. Your yard must be totally safe, with no vestige of any possible escape route. Remember that the Min Pin can be a great escape artist!

Bringing your puppy home means separating him from his mother, his siblings and the familiarity of the breeder's home. You will have to be reassuring and allow him some time to make the adjustment.

You should plan his diet with his breeder in advance; there is no better source of feeding advice than an experienced Min Pin breeder. You must also find out about the equipment you will need to buy. Discuss with the breeder exactly what your puppy will need to make his life healthy, safe and enjoyable.

Be prepared for your puppy to get into everything he can get his paws and teeth on! Missing your dish rag? Your pup might have a clue as to where you can find it.

Depending on where you live, you will probably have easy access to a good pet-supply store, either a large outlet or a privately owned shop. If you can find a store that is owned by people who show their own dogs, they often have a wide range of items and will probably be able to give sensible guidance as to what you need to buy. Major dog shows also usually have a wide range of trade stands that cater to every need, and you are sure to be absolutely spoiled by the excellent selection.

You will need some grooming equipment for your Miniature

Avoid giving your Min Pin a wicker bed, as the wicker is very tempting to a dog's teeth. Pieces can easily break off and be swallowed or otherwise injure the dog.

Pinscher puppy. You may need some different tools as your dog matures, but the Min Pin is not a high-maintenance breed. At this early stage, a grooming glove or a soft bristle brush will be your principal need. You will also need canine nail clippers. Certain things, like cotton balls, you probably already have in stock as household items.

Where your puppy is to sleep will be a major consideration, and you decide where this is going to be for the dog's life—not just for the "first few nights." Begin as you mean to go on. It is only natural that the newcomer will be restless and howl for the first couple of nights or so, but if you immediately take pity on the little soul and let him join you in your bedroom, he will expect to remain there always! Hence it is essential that the bedding you choose is soft and comfortable, so that your

puppy can rest and feel cozy in his special place.

Bearing in mind that a puppy will not want a bed that is too large, you may have to buy a very small one to begin with and then an adult-sized bed a few months later (which will not be too much larger than the puppy-sized bed). Wicker beds may look pretty, but they are dangerous because puppies chew them and sharp wicker pieces can all too easily injure eyes or be swallowed. It is wiser to choose a durable bed that can be washed or wiped down and can be lined with comfortable soft bedding that can be washed frequently. It will be important that all of your dog's bedding is kept clean and dry. You should also choose a bed that is just slightly raised from the ground or otherwise positioned so that it will avoid drafts.

The wire crate is a good tool for use in the home and outdoors, as it gives the dog a place of his own wherever you go and allows him a good view of what's going on around him.

Although a Miniature Pinscher is tiny, he can get into all kinds of mischief. Everyday household items may seem harmless enough, but a dainty cloth draped over the side of a little table full of fragile ornaments is asking for trouble! Even more dangerous to a mischievous puppy are electric cords, so be sure that they are totally out of his reach. Tiny teeth can bite though all too easily, causing what can be a fatal accident. Another word of warning concerns cleaning agents and fertilizers. Many of these contain substances that are poisonous, so please keep them out of the way of temptation. Dogs are attracted to the taste of antifreeze, but it only takes a drop or two to kill a dog of any size.

When your puppy first arrives home, it is only natural that you will be proud and will want to show your new companion to your friends. However, your puppy is making a big move in his short life, so the first two or three days are best spent quietly at home with you and your immediate family. When your puppy has begun to feel at home in his new surroundings and has received his second set of shots, you will be able to introduce him to lots of new people. If you have young children, or if they visit, always carefully supervise any time spent with your young puppy. Youngsters can all too easily hurt a small puppy, even with the sweetest of intentions.

If your family has other pets, introductions should be

Outdoor safety for your Min Pin includes a secure fence of appropriate height and making sure that there are no toxic plants or harmful chemicals.

made slowly and under close supervision. Most Miniature Pinschers get along well with other animals, but you should always exercise caution until you are certain that all concerned are going to be the best of friends. Of course, Min Pins don't appreciate sharing their homes with small-mammal-type pets, as their ratting instincts make this a very difficult friendship to forge. Some Min Pins will tolerate exotic birds, but even these must be carefully supervised and separated from the "Min Pin in charge."

In addition to his crate, your Min Pin will enjoy a soft dog bed or cushion on which to rest.

WELCOMING THE MIN PIN

Overview

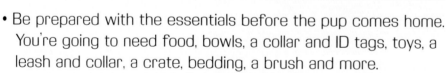

- Be prepared with the essentials before the pup comes home. You're going to need food, bowls, a collar and ID tags, toys, a leash and collar, a crate, bedding, a brush and more.
- Create a safe home for your puppy by removing hazards from the dog's environment indoors and out.
- Choose wisely when picking your pup's sleeping area, as this is where he should sleep throughout his life.
- Introductions between the pup and children and/or other pets must be done carefully and under supervision.

MINIATURE PINSCHER

House-training Your Puppy

Your Miniature Pinscher is an intelligent little dog, one that is perfectly capable of learning, but you can guarantee that there are times when he will misbehave. A Min Pin is very trainable and will quickly learn when he has done something wrong. If you have been sensible and consistent in your training, the chances are he will do it right the next time around. If not, with a little bit of luck, the following occasion will reap success. When you do need to correct him, this must be done in a

Small dogs like Min Pins can be trained to use a large cat litter box. If he is accustomed to using the box, you will need to take it with you when you travel, as this is what he will associate with toileting.

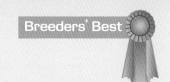

serious tone. To house-train success-fully, you will need to be firm, but never harsh, and you must certainly never be rough with your Miniature Pinscher.

When your puppy first arrives in your home he may or may not already be house-trained, albeit to a limited extent. However, you must always realize that your home is completely different from the breeder's, so he will have to relearn the house rules. Doors will not be located in the same places, your family may go to bed and rise at different times, and it will undoubtedly take him a little time to learn and to adapt.

The speed of your house-training success will depend to a certain extent on your own environment and to the season of the year. Most puppies are perfectly happy to go out into the yard in dry weather, but when it is pouring down rain, many

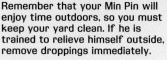

Remember that your Min Pin will enjoy time outdoors, so you must keep your yard clean. If he is trained to relieve himself outside, remove droppings immediately.

The best way to housebreak your Min Pin is to train him to "go" outside. If you do not have a yard, you will need to take him out frequently on his lead to do his business (don't forget the "poop-scoop!").

feel rather differently and will need considerable encouragement!

Paper training is always useful in the very early stages of training. Paper should be placed by the door so that the dog learns to associate the paper with the exit to the wide world outside. When he uses the paper, he should be praised. Obviously it is ideal if the puppy can be let out as soon as he shows any sign of wanting to do his toilet, but again this may depend on whether your home has immediate access to a yard.

Crate training is the housebreaking method of choice for most breeders and owners. The crate, which can be purchased from the pet-supply store, need only be the small wire type, which should last the life of the dog. This method is by far the most successful and is based on the dog's instinctive desire to keep his sleep-ing quarters clean. The golden rule "Don't toilet where you sleep" began with canines. The puppy should get in the habit of sleeping, resting and playing in his crate. He will soon learn to regard the crate as his own special place, "his room," if you will. The puppy should be taken out after nap periods and led to his toilet area in the yard. Lead him on his lead as opposed to carrying him—make him feel like a "big boy." Praise the dog when he does his business outdoors.

Remember that puppies need to go out much more frequently than adult dogs, certainly immediately after waking and following meals. In fact, to take your pup outside every hour while he is awake is not a bad idea at all. Always keep your eyes and ears open, for a youngster will not be able to wait those extra two or three minutes until it is convenient

Training includes setting the house rules and sticking to them. A Min Pin (or two!) on your couch will leave more than enough room for you, but you must decide if you want to allow your dog on the furniture.

for you to let him out. If you delay, accidents will certainly happen, so be warned!

The crate assists the pup in developing his muscles to "hold it." He has the strong desire not to relieve himself in his crate and thus learns to control his body's excretory muscles. He will look forward to the walk to the yard every time he's released from the crate.

As your puppy matures, "asking" to be let out when necessary will become second nature, and it will be very rare if you have a Min Pin that is unclean in the

Don't ignore the signs! If your Min Pin is waiting by the door, there is a reason.

house. A stud dog, however, can be different, for he may well want to mark his territory, and your table and chair legs may be just the places he decides to choose! Neutering a male puppy early will help tremendously in preventing marking behavior.

Simple one-word commands are very helpful; "Out" or "Potty" seem to work. Never, *ever* forget to give praise when the deed is done in the desired place. If an accident happens, you should indeed give a verbal reprimand, but this will only work if your Miniature Pinscher is caught in the act. If you try to reprimand him after the event, he will simply not know what he has done wrong and your scolding will only serve to confuse him.

It is essential that any mess is cleared up immediately, and if a dog has relieved himself in the wrong place, the area must be cleaned thoroughly to disguise the smell or he will want to use that particular place again. When your puppy is old enough to be exercised in public places, always carry with you a "pooper scoop" or small plastic bag so that any mess can be removed. The anti-dog lobby exists everywhere, so please give them no cause for complaint.

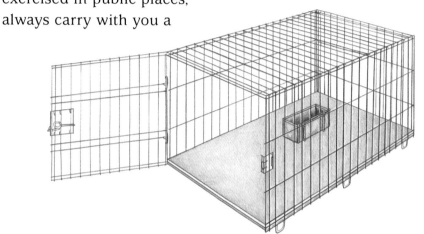

An adequately-sized wire crate will become your Min Pin's special den, an area that he will want to keep clean.

HOUSE-TRAINING YOUR PUPPY

Overview

- Essential for all puppy owners is house-training, teaching the dog proper toileting habits.
- The crate is the best answer to house-training your Miniature Pinscher. Learn how to use a crate correctly, never for punishment.
- Teach a relief command so that your puppy will always indicate when he needs to go out. Don't ignore his signs.
- As with all training, praise your dog when he does what you want. Only reprimand him for accidents if you catch him in the act.
- Paper training is an option for getting started with your Min Pin puppy, though it is surely not as reliable as crate training.

MINIATURE PINSCHER

Min Pin Puppy Training

Don't worry unduly if, when your Min Pin puppy arrives home, he appears less sure of himself than he was at the breeder's home.

Take into account that everything will be new to him. There will be no familiar sounds or smells, so he will need a little time to adapt to his new environment. He will look to you, as his owner, to give him confidence in these early stages of your time together.

Begin by getting him used to the members of your immediate family. Instilling confidence into your

There is nothing better than a crate for your Min Pin's safety during transport to training areas. You will find the crate useful in many situations throughout your dog's life.

Miniature Pinscher will help with his early socialization, something that is particularly important for a Min Pin. Soon you will be able to introduce him to your wider family and friends. Please try not to bombard him with too many new people and situations all at the same time.

Expose your Miniature Pinscher to the outside world once he's received all the necessary vaccinations. This young puppy is not quite ready to take his first big step.

Depending on the age of your puppy, and whether his course of vaccinations is complete, you may or may not be able to take him out in public places immediately. Whichever the case, I would still advise you to allow him to settle down at home for the first few days before venturing outside your home and yard. There will be lots you can do at home with your Miniature Pinscher puppy, so you will both undoubtedly have great fun, but you must allow him to get sufficient rest, too.

Early socialization begins before the pups go to new homes. Pups learn canine rules from their mother and become acclimated to interacting with humans by spending time with the breeder.

If he is restricted to your home territory for a little while, you can play games with him, using suitably safe, soft toys and not allowing him to tug on anything too strongly. Check regularly that sharp or unsafe parts, such as squeakers, do not become detached from the toys. These pieces can cause injury, and since your puppy's teeth will be very sharp, toys can easily be damaged. Soft toys are not recommended once the pup is past his teething stage. Instead, offer things like safe nylon bones and other sturdy toys. Always monitor the condition of all of your dog's toys.

Whether or not you plan to show your Miniature Pinscher, it is always good to do a little early training, getting him to stand calmly on a table to be groomed and admired. This will be helpful on many occasions, including during vet visits, when it is much easier to deal with a well-behaved dog. You will be so proud of your clever companion!

Accustom your puppy to being on a lead, which is always a strange experience for a tiny youngster. Begin by just putting a simple buckle collar on him, not too tightly, but not so loose that it can be caught on things, causing panic and possible injury. Just put it on for a few minutes at a time, lengthening each period slightly until your puppy feels comfortable in his first item of "clothing." Don't expect miracles; this may take a few days.

Then, when he is comfortable in the collar, attach a small lightweight nylon or cotton lead. The one you select must have a secure catch yet be simple to attach and release as necessary. Until now, your Miniature Pinscher puppy has simply gone where he has pleased and will find it very strange to be attached to someone restricting his movements. For this reason,

If your Min Pin puppy has been properly vaccinated and is ready to go out in public, socialization can begin. The pup will benefit from different sights, sounds, smells and experiences.

when training my own puppies, I like to allow them to "take" me for the first few sessions, after which I begin to exert a little pressure. Soon enough, training can start in earnest, with the puppy following me as I lead the way.

It is usual to begin training the puppy to walk on your left-hand side. When this has been accomplished to your satisfaction, you can try moving him on your right, but there is absolutely no hurry. If you plan to show your Miniature Pinscher, you will generally move your dog on your left, but sometimes (such as at a dog show) it is necessary also to move him on your right so as not to obstruct the judge's view.

As your puppy gets older you can teach him to sit, always using a simple one-word command, such as "Sit," while exerting a gentle push on his rump to show him what you expect. This will take a little time, but you will soon succeed. Always give plenty of praise when your pup assumes the sit position. Never shout or get angry when your dog does not achieve your aim, for this will do more harm than good. If yours is destined to be a show dog, you may decide not to teach him to sit, as he will be expected to stand in the show ring.

When your Miniature Pinscher puppy can venture out into public places, begin by taking him somewhere quiet without too much excitement. Soon you will find his confidence increasing and you can then introduce him to new places, with exciting sights, sounds and smells. He must always be on a safe lead that cannot be slipped (not the type used in the show ring).

When you have total confidence in one another,

You don't need a large crate to house your Min Pin comfortably. His small crate is easy to transport and will keep him safe during trips in the car—whether around the block or across the country!

you may be able to let him off lead, if this is permitted and you are in a securely enclosed area, but always keep him in sight. Be absolutely sure that the place you have chosen for free exercise is completely safe and that no strange dogs can suddenly appear from "nowhere!"

We have discussed the benefits of crate training the puppy for house-training, but there are other advantages to the crate, including training, traveling and general care and safety. Crate training pays off for pet and show dog alike. At dog shows, most dogs (and all toy breeds) are housed in crates for at least part of the time while awaiting their turn to be exhibited in the ring. Crates are also useful for keeping a dog safe while traveling. In the home, most dogs seem to look upon their crates as safe places to go and don't mind staying there for short periods of time. This can be helpful in times when you cannot supervise or when there's a lot going on in the house and you don't want your Min Pin to be underfoot.

When you commence crate training, Place your pup in his crate and remain within his sight. Give him a toy or something to occupy his mind. To begin, leave him in the crate for very short spells of just a minute or two, then gradually build up the timespan. However, never confine a dog to a crate for long periods, for that would be unkind. Most dogs can remain crated for

A future star is guided into the "stack," which is the standing pose used in the show ring. Training for potential show dogs begins early.

their nighttime sleep periods and for a few hours during the day.

Another positive aspect of crate training is that it provides a place for your dog to rest when he's sick or under the weather. If the vet recommends "bed rest" for your Min Pin, you can put him to bed in his crate. Dogs that are not crate-trained cannot be so easily confined for such purposes. After spaying or neutering your Min Pin, or if he has to have any other minor surgery (such as cataract or

Show dogs are trained to "stack" on a table for the judge's examination. Practice your Min Pin's show stance at home, using your grooming table.

patellar surgery), the crate serves as the ideal "get well" ward. What better place to recuperate than a special place of his own?

MIN PIN PUPPY TRAINING

Overview

- A key to your Min Pin's becoming well adjusted is socialization. Once he has been properly vaccinated, you can introduce your pup to the world outside your home.
- Early training includes introducing your pup to his collar and lead and giving him time to become comfortable wearing them.
- Consider your Min Pin's safety when out in public places.
- The crate is more than just an effective house-training tool. Explore its many uses and benefits for your dog's general care and safety.

MINIATURE PINSCHER

Teaching Basic Commands

Because your Miniature Pinscher is intelligent and highly alert, he is a prime candidate for learning new skills. He will enjoy following your commands, but you must always be consistent in your training. You will need to keep in mind that the Min Pin is renowned for playing the court jester, so you might find that sometimes he'd rather play a trick on you than do what is required of him.

Although some show dogs are trained in obedience, many

Be sure to take time out of your training for playtime! A dog is more likely to cooperate with his lessons if he associates them with something fun.

exhibitors feel this can be detrimental to a dog's performance in the show ring, so you will have to bear this in mind if you plan to show. Regardless, all dogs must be taught basic good manners; the way you go about this may be slightly different with a future show dog.

In all training, it is essential to get your dog's full attention, which many owners do with the aid of treats so that the dog learns to associate treats with praise (positive reinforcement). The following training method involves using food treats, although eventually you will wean your dog off these training aids so that your rewards are based on praise with an occasional treat. Always use very simple commands, just one or two short words. Keep sessions short so they do not become boring for your dog. It's important to have your dog's undivided attention to be successful with your lessons.

Scolding may be necessary from time to time, but your training method should be one based on positive reinforcement, using praise and treats as motivators and rewards.

"Sit" is the first command you will teach to your Min Pin. The dog may need to be guided into position at first, but he should understand what is expected of him after a few tries.

CHAPTER 9

SIT

With the lead in your left hand, hold a small treat in your right, letting your dog smell or lick the treat but not take it. Move it away as you say "Sit," your hand rising slowly over the dog's head so that he looks upward. In doing so, he will bend his knees and sit. When he assumes the proper position, give him the food reward and lavish praise.

HEEL

A dog trained to walk at heel will walk alongside his handler without pulling. Again the lead should be held in your left hand while the dog assumes the sit position next to your left leg. Hold the end of the lead in your right hand, but also control it lower down with your left.

Step forward with your right foot, saying "Heel." To begin, just take three steps, then command him to sit again. Repeat this procedure until he carries out the task without pulling. Then you can increase the number of strides to five, seven and so on. Give verbal praise at the close of each section of the exercise and, at the end of the training session, let him enjoy himself with a free run in the fenced yard.

It's no use training if your Min Pin is looking away from you, distracted by something he finds more interesting. Get and keep your dog's attention, and keep lessons short and positive. Dogs get bored just as we do!

DOWN

When your dog is proficient in sitting, you can introduce the "Down." It is essential from the onset to understand that a dog will consider the down position as a submissive one, so gentle training is important. Your confident, cocky Min Pin will not instantly assume this position, so take your time and be patient. Remember, you are the one who is "top dog" in this relationship, not your perky pal.

With your Miniature Pinscher sitting by your left leg, as for the sit, hold the lead in your left hand and a treat in your right. Place your left hand on top of the dog's shoulders (without pushing) and hold the treat under his nose, saying "Down" in a quiet tone of voice. Gradually move the treat along the floor, in front of the dog, all the while talking gently. He will follow that treat, lowering himself down. When his elbows touch the floor, you can

Heel training is necessary for all dogs, no matter their size. It's unlikely that your Min Pin will drag you down the street, but his good manners are important in all that you do together.

release the treat and give praise, but try to get him to remain there for a few seconds before getting up. Gradually the time of the down exercise can be increased.

STAY

The "stay" can be taught with your dog in either a sit or a down position, as usual with the lead in your left hand and the treat in your right. Allow him to lick the treat as you say "Stay" while standing directly in front of the dog, having moved from your position beside him.

Silently count to about five, then move back to your original position alongside the dog, allowing him to have the treat while giving him lavish praise.

Keep practicing the stay just as described for a few days, then gradually increase the distance between you. Along with

To begin the down/stay, have the dog assume the down position by your left side before you step out in front of him.

Once he will stay with you right in front of him, gradually increase the distance and time. Your palm facing him as a "stop" sign reinforces your verbal command to "Stay."

your verbal command, use your hand with the palm facing the dog as an indication that he must stay. Soon you should be able to do this exercise off lead (in a safe area), and your Miniature Pinscher will stay for increasingly longer periods of time. Always give lavish praise upon completion of the exercise.

Show dogs, of course, practice the stay command in a standing or "stacked" position. Exhibitors must keep their dogs standing perfectly still (in a stay) while the judge observes them in the line-up and individually. Most Min Pins naturally assume a proud stacked position. An experienced exhibitor can advise you about the proper stance for the Min Pin, with his feet planted firmly on the ground, his neck handsomely arched and his head held high (as all Min Pins' heads should be!).

RECALL (COME)

Your Miniature Pinscher will love to come back to you when called, thus the term "recall." The idea is to recall him, or invite him to return, offering a treat and giving lots of praise when he does so. It is important to teach the recall, for this should bring your dog running back to you if ever he is danger of moving out of sight. Most trainers use the command "Come" for this purpose.

When calling your dog to you, be sure you sound upbeat and happy, as the Min Pin is far too smart to come back to you if you sound as if you want to wring his neck for chewing your Gucci shoes! Does it need to be said that you never practice this command (or any other command) when you're in a sour mood or angry with the dog? Training has to remain positive—for both parties.

TRICKS

The Miniature Pinscher is a wonderful little character and may enjoy learning a trick or two. After all, he

Once your dog is proficient in the basic commands, you can take your training to the next level with an activity. Agility is a popular sport that you can begin once your dog reaches one year of age. Navigating the obstacles will give your athletic Min Pin a mental and physical workout.

loves to be the center of attention and is a crowd-pleaser! What you teach will be a matter of choice, but some dogs learn to offer their paws, and others like to sit up and "beg," which is particularly enchanting. Treats and your delight should be enough to teach the talented Min Pin just about any trick. Have fun with your Min Pin's training and the rewards will keep on coming. How about a high-five from your prancing little housemate?

He will never admit it, but your Min Pin needs and wants discipline! He will thank you for the time you put into his education, and the relationship will be a rewarding one for both of you.

TEACHING BASIC COMMANDS

Overview

- Begin basic obedience training on the right paw. Keep lessons short and positive, using treats and praise to motivate and reward your Min Pin.
- Choose a safely enclosed area for your lessons.
- The sit exercise is the first you will teach and serves as a basis for other exercises.
- The down command may take more time, as this is not a natural position for Min Pins.
- A reliable recall, or "come," is essential to your Min Pin's safety.
- Your playful Min Pin will delight you with his aptitude for tricks.

MINIATURE PINSCHER

Home Care for Your Min Pin

A healthy Min Pin generally lives for 12 to 14 years, sometimes even longer. Obviously, if your dog enjoys good health, the chances of a long lifespan are considerably increased. In knowing and understanding your Min Pin well, you will be able to pick up on any signs he may give you that he is not feeling his usual sprightly self. This will help you to see problems arising so that you can take your pet to the vet without delay for further investigation.

Using a doggy-formulated toothpaste and soft brush, make tooth-cleaning part of your Min Pin's regular grooming routine.

DENTAL CARE

Keeping teeth in good condition is your responsibility. You owe this to your dog, for dental problems do not stop inside the mouth. When gums are infected, all sorts of health problems can subsequently arise, with the infection spreading through the system and possibly leading even to death.

Aside from brushing his teeth, also inspect your Min Pin's overall mouth and gum condition.

You may clean your Miniature Pinscher's teeth extremely gently and carefully, using a very small tooth-brush and special canine toothpaste. Take particular care if any of the puppy teeth are beginning to loosen. Your dog may not like this procedure much at first, but he should easily get used to it if you clean his teeth regularly. Experienced breeders sometimes use a special dental scraper, but damage can be done with this, especially on a toy breed, so I do not recommended it for use by the average pet owner.

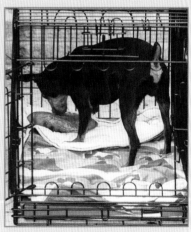
Safe chew toys aid in keeping a dog's teeth free of tartar. Be careful with rawhide, because even the largest chews will eventually soften, and can be swallowed and choke the dog.

CHAPTER 10

When cleaning the teeth, always check the gums for signs of inflammation. If you notice that the gums look red or swollen, a visit to your vet would be worthwhile.

FIRST AID

Accidents can happen and, if they do, you must remain as cool, calm and collected as possible under the circumstances. You will be able to think more clearly (and find

A big part of your Min Pin's everyday care is keeping him safe and secure. Don't underestimate his climbing, jumping and digging skills when erecting a proper fence or confining him in a wire pen.

this page in the book) if you are not overreacting to finding a tick on your Min Pin's head or discovering the fertilizer bag mysteriously empty.

Insect stings are quite frequent. If it is still there, the "stinger" should be removed with tweezers. Ice can be applied to reduce the swelling and an accurate dosage of antihistamine (consult your vet!) treatment given. If a sting is inside the mouth, consult your vet at once.

Accidental poisoning is also a worry, as dogs can investigate all sorts of things, not all of which are safe. If you suspect poisoning, try to ascertain the cause, because treatment may vary according to the type of poison ingested. Vomiting or sudden bleeding from an exit point, such as the gums, can be indications of poisoning. Immediate veterinary attention is essential.

Small abrasions should be cleaned thoroughly and

antiseptic applied. In the case of serious bleeding, initially apply pressure above the area. For minor burns, apply cool water.

In the case of shock, such especially over the shoulders. In severe cases, the dog should be submerged in water up to his neck if possible. Dogs can die quickly from heat stroke, so

A group of sun-seekers, enjoying the warmth and fresh air. In sunny weather, dogs should always have access to shade and plenty of cool water to avoid the dangers of heat stroke.

as following a car accident, keep the dog warm while veterinary aid is sought without delay. Do not move the dog unless absolutely necessary.

For heat stroke, cold water must be applied immediately, immediate veterinary attention is of paramount importance. Conversely, in the case of hypothermia, keep the dog warm with hot-water bottles and give a warm bath, if possible, while contacting the veterinarian.

Be observant of your Min Pin's behavior around the home to ensure that he's always acting like his healthy, happy, alert self.

RECOGNIZING HEALTH SIGNS

If you love your Miniature Pinscher and you spend plenty of time together, you will know when something is amiss. He may go off his food or seem dull and listless. His eyes, usually bright and alive, may seem to have lost their sparkle, and his coat may look more dull than usual.

His potty habits may also be an indication of ill health. Loose movements usually clear up within 24 hours, but if they go on for longer than this, especially if you see blood, you will need to visit your vet. Also keep a lookout for increased thirst and an increase in frequency of urination, which could indicate a medical problem.

CHECKING FOR PARASITES

It is essential to keep your dog's coat in top condition. Be on guard against parasites, which can be a nuisance and cause irritation to your Min Pin's skin. It is often not easy to see parasites, but if you catch sight of even one flea, you can be sure that there are more lurking somewhere. There are now several good preventive aids available for external parasites, and your vet will be able to advise you about these. In some countries, the best remedies are available only from the veterinarian.

Also be on the continual lookout for ear mites. These cannot be seen, but a brown discharge, with some odor from the ear, is a clear indication that they are present. A suitable ear treatment will be available from your vet.

Be aware that many dog maladies are easily transmitted from dog to dog, so be familiar with the other canines with which your Min Pin spends time.

CHAPTER 10

A dog can also carry internal parasites in the form of worms. Ascarids are the most common and tapeworms, although less frequent, can be even more debilitating.

your vet. Given the prevalence of heartworm in the US, it is wise to begin heartworm prevention at eight weeks of age, regardless of where you live. Preventives

Parasites, allergens, stinging insects and other irritants are lurking out there, but that doesn't mean you should deny your Min Pin time outside. Rather, just be diligent in checking his skin and coat for any signs of trouble.

Heartworms are transmitted by mosquitoes and prove to be fatal to dogs. Discuss a heartworm preventive program with

can be taken monthly or every second or third month, depending on the type selected. Since the heartworm medication can poison the worms at any stage of growth, even a monthly preventive can be taken every third month and still serve the purpose of keeping your dog heartworm-free. It only stands to reason that owners want to feed their dogs "bug poison" as infrequently as possible. Your vet may disagree with the author on this matter, but, in any case, be sure to weigh the pros and cons when deciding on a safe course of prevention for your Min Pin.

There is no argument here: routine worming is essential throughout a dog's life and veterinary recommendation as to a suitable regime is certainly advised. Don't be too smart when visiting your vet or you may create an adversarial relationship between you and him (and your innocent, lovable Min Pin). It's vital that you establish a friendly but intelligent rapport with your vet. He'll respect you more knowing that you care enough to be knowledgeable and responsible about your dog's care.

HOME CARE FOR YOUR MIN PIN

Overview

- Dental care should be an important part of your Min Pin's home-care routine. Plaque accumulation and the diseases associated with it can cause serious health problems.
- Know the signs of emergency and first-aid procedures.
- During weekly grooming sessions, keep an eye on the condition of your Min Pin's skin and coat.
- Know the signs of wellness and the symptoms of disease so that you can recognize when your Min Pin's health may be compromised.
- Discuss a safe worming routine with your vet.

MINIATURE PINSCHER

Feeding Your Min Pin

Your Miniature Pinscher is likely to enjoy his food, but never allow him to become overweight. Excess weight will be easy to spot on a smooth-coated small breed like the Min Pin. Min Pins have (or *should* have) a waist! Overweight dogs are more prone to health problems than dogs that are kept in good weight and condition. There will be additional strain on the heart and joints, and there will be increased risk when the dog is under anesthesia. Since the Min Pin is naturally active, you

The breeder starts the litter off with a quality puppy food and will be a helpful source of advice about how to continue feeding your Min Pin, including changing feeding schedules and amounts, and switching to adult food as your puppy matures.

should have no problem keeping him fit and trim if you feed a sensible, balanced diet.

Today there is an enormous range of specially prepared foods available for dogs, many of them scientifically balanced and geared toward specific age ranges (puppy, juniors, adults and seniors). It is really a matter of personal preference as to which brand of food you decide to feed, though initially this will be influenced by the brand and type of food that has been fed to your new puppy by his breeder. Changes can, of course, be made to the puppy's diet once you bring him home. Never, however, change suddenly from one food to another, or your Miniature Pinscher is likely to get an upset tummy. Introduce a new brand of food gradually over a few days until the old brand is phased out. There is usually no harm at all in changing the flavor of food while keeping with

Water is just as important to your dog's diet as proper nutrition. Have clean, cool, fresh water available to your Min Pin at all times.

With the lean and muscular Min Pin, it will be easy to see if your dog puts on a few pounds (or even ounces).

the same brand. This can add some variety to the diet. You might prefer to add a little flavored stock to tempt the dog's palate.

Once you have decided upon the brand of food to offer your Min Pin, make sure that you thoroughly read the feeding instructions as to the amount of food appropriate for a dog the size of your Min Pin. Additionally, some foods recommend that they be soaked before offering them to the dog, especially those foods for youngsters. Because your Min Pin is tiny, you would be well advised to purchase the kibble labeled "small bite," made especially for miniature mouths.

Dry food should also be stored carefully, bearing in mind that its vitamin value declines if not used fairly quickly, usually within about three months. It is essential that a plentiful supply of fresh water is available for your dog when feeding dry foods in

particular, though dogs should, of course, have access to water at all times, regardless of what type of diet is fed.

Because of the enormous range of products available, you may find it difficult to decide which to choose without advice from your breeder or another Miniature Pinscher enthusiast. However, keep in mind that in adulthood, an active dog will require a higher protein content than one that lives a sedentary life.

Despite the major advances in canine nutrition by manufacturers, some owners still prefer to feed fresh foods. If you are interested in exploring this option, you must be certain that you know how to prepare and feed a well-balanced, nutritionally complete diet. There currently seems to be a move toward reverting back to the more natural diet of the wild. Some owners even give raw chicken wings, which dogs seem to

A quality commercial dog food should contain all of the nutrients that a dog needs, in proper proportions and balance.

thoroughly enjoy, although you must never feed cooked chicken bones. Many say this helps to keep teeth clean and breath fresh. Cooked vegetables are also beneficial to this type of diet. A word of caution, though: Be sure that no dangerous things like cooked bones of any type are included in your Min Pin's meals.

Many owners are tempted to feed treats frequently between meals, but this is not a good idea. Overdoing it with treats will cause weight to pile on almost imperceptibly. A very suitable alternative is to give the occasional piece of carrot. Most dogs love them! Carrots don't put on any weight and are another useful

Whether taking a road trip or enjoying a day out at a show, bring along all of the accessories that you and your Min Pin will need, including his crate, food, water and bowls.

aid to keeping the teeth clean. No dog should be fed chocolate of the kind that humans eat, as this is carcinogenic to dogs. Onions are another "people food" toxic to dogs.

How many times a day you feed your adult Miniature Pinscher will probably be a matter of personal preference. Many feed just once each day, but others prefer to feed two smaller meals daily. Like young babies, puppies need to be fed more frequently than adults, but your dog's breeder will give you good advice in this regard, and the transition from the puppy to adult feeding schedule will be made gradually.

As a dog gets older, his metabolism changes and thus feeding requirements may change. A typical change is from one meal a day to two or even three smaller ones. By then you will know your pet well and should be able to adjust his feeding accordingly. If you have any queries, your vet will be able to guide you in the right direction.

FEEDING YOUR MIN PIN

Overview

- Quality counts when feeding any dog. Offering a top-quality dog food is the most reliable and convenient way to provide complete nutrition for your Miniature Pinscher.
- Discuss with your vet and/or breeder the amount to feed your Min Pin. Also take advice about feeding schedules and dietary changes at each stage of life.
- If you are interested in feeding a fresh-food diet, you must be thoroughly educated as to how to do this correctly for proper nutrition and health.
- A treat is a welcome reward, but don't overdo it!

MINIATURE PINSCHER

Grooming Your Min Pin

The Miniature Pinscher has a short coat, so grooming is minimal compared to that of many other breeds. Nonetheless, coat care is an essential part of canine maintenance and the grooming procedure can be pleasurable for both dog and owner. Grooming will almost undoubtedly strengthen the bond between you and your dog. Ideally your Miniature Pinscher will be groomed on a firm table with a non-slip surface. A grooming table, available from your pet store, is ideal for the dog (and for

The Min Pin's short coat doesn't require fancy grooming to keep it looking its sleek, shiny best.

your soon-to-be-aching back if you attempt to crouch down to groom your tiny dog). You will find that Miniature Pinscher owners use slightly different pieces of equipment, according to what they find suits best. You will hopefully get good advice from the breeder about grooming when you discuss your new puppy's care. Once you become experienced with grooming, you will develop your own preferences.

Too-frequent bathing can strip a dog of his natural oils, leaving the skin and coat dry. In between baths, a damp cloth over the coat is a good way to freshen up.

COAT CARE

It is essential to keep your Min Pin's coat clean and to groom regularly. Many people feel it is unwise to bathe the dog too frequently because this can tend to dry out the coat. However, it is always wise to check the skin and coat every day so that no unexpected problems start to develop.

A handy grooming tool is a brush that's made to fit on your hand.

Most people use a grooming glove or a soft bristle brush, both of which will help to remove any loose hair. A brisk brush-through will help your Min Pin maintain his clean, shiny coat.

Grooming will also massage and stimulate the skin. Even massaging with your hand in the direction of coat growth helps to keep the coat glossy. Some people like to use a chamois leather or piece of velvet for the finishing touch.

BATHING YOUR MINIATURE PINSCHER

When you decide to bathe your Min Pin, it will not be a major event, for this breed is small enough to bathe in the sink if you prefer not to use the bathtub. If a Miniature Pinscher puppy is accustomed to being bathed from a young age, he will be perfectly happy to accept this part of the grooming routine as he grows older.

Always brush your Miniature Pinscher's coat thoroughly before bathing, then stand your dog on a non-slip surface. Be sure to test the water temperature on the back of your own hand. Use a canine shampoo, not a human one, taking care not to get water into eyes or ears. It is usually wise to wash the head last so that shampoo does not drip into the eyes while you are concentrating on another part of the body. Take care to reach all the slightly awkward places, so that no area is neglected.

Carefully lift your Miniature Pinscher out of the sink or bath wrapped in a warm, clean towel. Then dry your dog thoroughly with a towel or a blow dryer, remembering that dogs do not like air blowing toward their faces. Also remember that the Min Pin has a short coat and that a dog's skin is sensitive, so use a dryer on only the lowest heat, held at a good distance from the dog. Keep him indoors and away from drafts until he is completely dry.

As an alternative to bathing, you can wipe your Min Pin down with a washcloth dampened with plain warm water. This a favored way of keeping the coat clean without taking out too much oil, as can be the case with frequent bathing. You should begin with the face, where you will need to pay special attention to the area under the eyes. You will then work backwards to the tail. There will be no harm in doing this every few days, just as long as you make sure your dog is completely dry before going outdoors.

EARS AND EYES

It is important to keep your Miniature Pinscher's eyes and ears clean. They should be carefully wiped, perhaps using one of the proprietary cleaners available from good pet stores. If your dog has been shaking his head or scratching at his ears, there may well be an infection or ear mites. A thick brown discharge and bad smell can also mean problems, so get to the vet right away.

At any sign of injury to

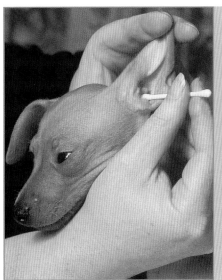

The Min Pin's upright ears are open to dirt and debris. Regular ear-cleaning and inspection are important, but it's safer to use a cotton ball or other soft wipe rather than a cotton swab, which poses the danger of entering the ear canal and causing injury.

the eye, or if the eye turns blue, veterinary attention must be sought immediately. If an eye injury is dealt with quickly, it can often be repaired; if neglected, however, it can lead to loss of sight.

Chapter 12

NAILS AND FEET

Nails must always be kept short, but how frequently they need clipping depends very much on the surfaces upon which your dog walks. Min Pins living their lives primarily on carpets or on grass will need more frequent attention to their nails than those who are walked regularly on pavement.

Your Miniature Pinscher should be trained to accept nail clipping from an early age. Take great care not to cut into the quick, which is the blood vessel that runs through the nail. Your Min Pin will let you know when you've cut into his quick—when a Min Pin screams, you remember it! It is a good idea to keep a styptic pencil or some styptic powder on hand to stop the flow of blood in case of accident. Cutting just a small sliver of nail at a time

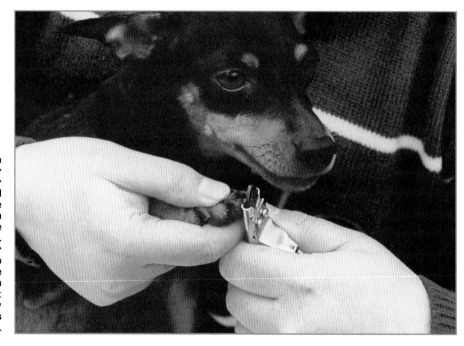

Purchase a nail clipper made for dogs and introduce your Min Pin to it when he is still young. Getting your pup used to the procedure will result in an adult that sits pretty for his pedicures.

is the safest approach. You should also inspect the feet regularly to be sure that nothing has become wedged or embedded between the pads.

ANAL GLANDS

A dog's anal glands are located on either side of the anal opening. Sometimes they become blocked and require evacuation. Experienced breeders often do this themselves, but pet owners would be well advised to leave this to their vet, for damage can be caused and evacuation is not always necessary. Firm stools help to evacuate the anal glands naturally, so diet will have a bearing on this.

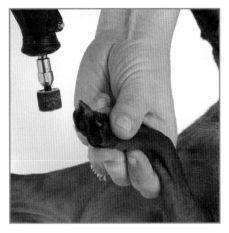

Some owners prefer to use an electric grinder for keeping their dogs' nails short. It's a matter of personal preference. Some dogs don't mind the grinder, while others don't seem to like the noise or feel of it.

GROOMING YOUR MIN PIN

Overview

- While the Min Pin is a low-maintenance dog when it comes to grooming, proper coat care is a vital part of his overall health-care program and must be initiated when the pup is young.
- Grooming includes taking care of the dog's coat as well as nails, feet, ears, eyes and anal glands.
- You will only have to bathe your Min Pin occasionally, as too-frequent bathing dries out the skin and coat.
- When dealing with ear or eye problems, owners must not wait too long to seek treatment. Early treatment can mean the difference between a quick recovery and the development of serious problems.

MINIATURE PINSCHER

Keeping the Min Pin Active

Your Miniature Pinscher is sure to be a highly inquisitive little dog who will love to investigate new places and new smells. In doing this, his senses will remain alert.

Although small, your Min Pin will need exercise to keep him in the peak of physical and mental condition.

Some Miniature Pinschers, when trained, are fairly obedient off lead, but you must keep foremost in your mind that this is a very small breed. Accidents could happen all too easily if he runs off

Conformation showing is one of the most popular activities for pure-bred dogs, especially among the Miniature Pinscher set.

to follow his nose or if larger dogs are encountered. For this reason, when out in public places, most Min Pin owners should keep their dogs on leads or even under the arm. Min Pins may be smaller than Dobermans, but no one has ever told them so! Keep your miniature dog's "big-dog" head in check.

Unless your Miniature Pinscher is used to children, he might also take exception to toddlers approaching him unexpectedly, so you must be alert about all that's going on when out walking. Once returning home, it is important that your Min Pin does not remain damp if you've been out in inclement weather.

If you have more than one Miniature Pinscher, they will provide each other with exercise by playing together. If yours is an "only child," you will be his favorite playmate. Lots of fun and amusement can be found around your house and yard.

Obstacles like the agility tunnel are no problem for the Min Pin, who uses his body and brains to learn to conquer the course.

If you have a fenced yard, your Min Pin will get a lot of exercise by running, playing and exploring. Of course, his favorite exercise will be activities that he does with you!

Miniature Pinscher

CHAPTER 13

Some Miniature Pinschers are now used in therapy work, visiting nursing homes and hospitals. The breed's convenient size and buoyant personality make these visits something to which hospital patients and the elderly greatly look forward. It is also not unknown for a Miniature Pinscher to become a hearing dog, assisting the deaf in their day-to-day lives. This is a dog that is especially trained to

When it's time for a walk, your energetic Min Pin will always be ready to go.

Occupy your Min Pin with safe, interesting toys. Remember, a bored dog will find ways to keep himself busy, and these likely will be ways of which you will not approve.

listen for sounds like telephones and doorbells ringing, something of great assistance to an owner with impaired hearing.

Always on their toes in mind and body, Miniature Pinschers take part in obedience trials. If well trained, they can really excel in this field. The small Miniature Pinscher may not spring immediately to mind when you think of agility trials. However, toy dogs frequently participate in these trials, of course on courses where the obstacles have been reduced in size according to the size of the dogs. The Min Pin could never outrun a Border Collie, but he certainly can give a Pomeranian or Papillon a run for their money!

Even if your Miniature Pinscher does not take part in any of these activities, you can enjoy endless hours of fun together. He will always love a game with a suitably safe toy. Remember always to check toys regularly to ensure that no loose parts might cause accidental damage.

The Min Pin is a loyal dog who enjoys time with his owner and will anxiously await your return home. If you are out at work during the day, don't neglect your dog when you come home. Always make time for your Min Pin!

KEEPING THE MIN PIN ACTIVE

Overview

- Daily walks give your Min Pin exercise, while the sights and sounds of the neighborhood will stimulate his brain.
- "On lead only" is a good rule of thumb for your Min Pin's safety when out in public.
- A Min Pin's talents can be put to good use by participating in therapy or assistance work.
- Participating in dog shows, obedience competitions and agility trials are excellent forums for dog and owner.
- Don't forget that the best activity for a Min Pin is anything done with his favorite person—you!

MINIATURE PINSCHER

Your Min Pin and His Vet

With a pint-sized dog like the Min Pin, visiting the vet is much less hassle than maneuvering a giant like the Great Dane into a congested waiting room. You will be able to carry your dog under your arm or you may prefer to use his crate or a lightweight carrying case. Do not put your dog on the floor. Remember that he may be a little tense in the vet's office, especially if he is feeling a bit under the weather.

You love your Miniature Pinscher, so show him by always providing for his veterinary care and maintenance of optimal health.

If you do not already have a vet for other family pets, you should select this new family professional very carefully. Preferably take recommendations from someone who has dogs of his own and whose opinion you trust. Location is also an important factor, for you must be able to get your dog there quickly in an emergency and the vet must be able to respond rapidly when needed. If you live in a rural area, please be sure that you choose a vet who has plenty of dealings with pet animals, preferably small breeds. Many have a great deal of experience with farm animals, but sadly their experience with dogs is limited, something I have learned the hard way in the past.

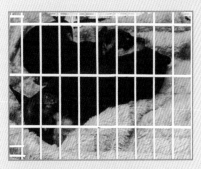

Breeders have to be diligent in providing the pups with good care, clean living quarters and attention to their health at this crucial young age.

An adult Min Pin and a senior member of the breed enjoy some time outdoors.

VACCINATIONS

You will have to take your puppy to the vet to complete his course of vaccination and to follow up with his boosters. You will want to review the inoculation schedule with your vet when you bring the puppy there for his initial visit. Set up an appointment for your puppy within the first few days of acquiring him. Most breeders will allow you a few days to untreatable or life-threatening, the breeder will take the puppy back.

Routine vaccinations vary slightly depending upon where you live and the type of vaccine used by your particular vet. Your vet

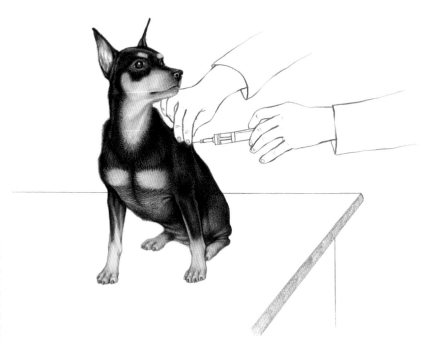

Your vet will manage your Min Pin's vaccination schedule from his puppy shots to his booster-shot program.

have the puppy checked out, guaranteeing the pup's health. In the odd case that the vet recognizes some malady in the puppy that is will advise you exactly about timing, such as when your dog can be exercised in public places after the course is complete and when boosters are due. Many vets now send reminder notices for boosters, but you should still make a note on your calendar. If you are visiting your vet for an initial vacci-nation program, do not allow your dog to come into close contact with other dogs in the waiting room!

Some people prefer not to subject their animals to routine vaccinations, but opt for a homeopathic alter-native. This needs to be carried out to the letter, so you must be guided be a vet who also practices homeopathy. Also bear in mind that it will probably be difficult to find a boarding kennel that accepts a dog without proof of a routine vaccination program.

PREVENTATIVE CARE

If your puppy has been bought from a truly dedicated breeder, all necessary care will have been provided not only for the litter but also for the dam. She will have had regular health checkups and boosters, with a worming

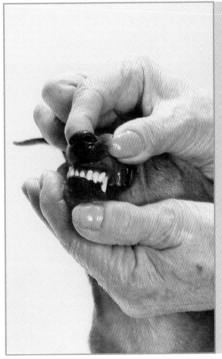

Dental health is very important. Your vet should examine your Min Pin's teeth as part of his routine check-ups; he may also perform a thorough veterinary tooth-scraping.

routine. These will stand her puppies in good stead and provide them with greater immunity than would otherwise be the case.

It is also of great impor-tance that any recommended tests for genetic abnormalities were carried out prior to the mating. A genuinely caring breeder will only have bred from a sound, healthy bitch, free of genetic disorders, and will have selected a stud dog of similar quality.

Graying on the muzzle is one of the first symptoms of a dog's aging. Seniors need to take life more slowly, but will still enjoy being included in their owners' activities.

CHECKUPS

When your Miniature Pinscher goes along to the vet for booster vaccinations, your vet will also give a brief routine health check. If the vet you use does not do this as a matter of course, request that the heart is checked while you visit, especially if your dog is past middle age. In addition to visits for boosters, your Min Pin should visit the vet each year for a thorough exam, including a dental evaluation and any necessary routine tests.

NEUTERING AND SPAYING

Whether or not you decide to have your dog spayed is a matter of personal choice. It is best to spay your bitch after her first season. Timing "mid-season" will usually be advised.

Spaying pet female dogs prevents various diseases such as breast cancer, uterine and ovarian cancer. All pet

Good health
starts with
good
breeding, the
principle of
every ethical
breeder.

owners should heed this warning for the continued good health of their Min Pins.

Should you opt for neutering your male dog or spaying your bitch, you will have to take special care with subsequent weight control. In many cases, an aggressive or over-dominant male can be easier to cope with after neutering.

Obviously there are some reasons of ill health that necessitate such operations, particularly pyometra, which will usually require a bitch's uterus and ovaries to be removed. In the case of a male with only one or neither testicle descended into the scrotum, your vet may well advise castration to prevent the likelihood of cancer. Discuss all pros and cons of the procedure with your vet to help you make a decision.

YOUR MIN PIN AND HIS VET

Overview

- Choose a qualified vet, located conveniently, who is experienced in caring for small dogs. Take your Min Pin puppy to the vet within the first few days of bringing him home.
- Discuss a vaccination schedule with your vet and be sure to keep your regular appointments for completing your dog's puppy shots and for his boosters.
- Don't allow your Min Pin to come into contact with other dogs before his vaccinations are complete or if he's not feeling well.
- Practice preventative medicine to keep your dog in healthy condition and prevent the occurrence of illness.
- Discuss neutering/spaying with your vet.